Living
on a
Ranch

by Christian Downey

illustrated by
Martin Lemelman

Scott Foresman
is an imprint of

Glenview, Illinois • Boston, Massachusetts • Chandler, Arizona
Upper Saddle River, New Jersey

Photographs

Every effort has been made to secure permission and provide appropriate credit for photographic material. The publisher deeply regrets any omission and pledges to correct errors called to its attention in subsequent editions.

Unless otherwise acknowledged, all photographs are the property of Pearson Education, Inc.

Photo locators denoted as follows: Top (T), Center (C), Bottom (B), Left (L), Right (R), Background (Bkgd)

20 (BC) Library of Congress, (BL) Pictorial Press Ltd/Alamy Images, (BR) Prints & Photographs Division, LC-USZ62-82912/Library of Congress.

Illustrations Martin Lemelman.

ISBN 13: 978-0-328-51341-3
ISBN 10:   0-328-51341-5

7 8 9 10 11 V010 17 16 15 14 13

Maria and Angela Ramirez are sisters who live on a ranch out West with their mother and father. Their Uncle Leo also lives on the ranch and helps the family with all of the work. On the ranch they grow crops, such as wheat and corn. They also have many animals, such as chickens, horses, and dogs. The girls even have their very own pigs!

Living on a ranch is hard work, and everyone has to help. Maria and Angela's grandmother helps feed the cows when she visits. She also makes big lunches for the family to eat. Maria and Angela love to help their grandmother cook. They also like to help their parents with the work. There is so much to do on the ranch!

Maria and Angela have always lived on the ranch where their father grew up. Some nights before bed, he tells the girls stories about when he was a child.

"Did you have your own animals, Papi?" asks Angela curiously.

"I sure did," he answers. "We had cows and horses, and I had my very own dog."

"Did you drive a tractor when you were little?" questions Maria.

"Not until I grew up," laughs their father. "And you are not old enough to drive yet either!" he winks.

Maria and Angela both can't wait to drive the tractor, but they know they are still too young.

Sometimes it rains at the ranch. Maria and Angela's parents are happy when it rains because rain helps the crops grow. If the crops don't get enough rain, they might die. The Ramirezes plant the crops in the spring and hope for good weather.

The climate is mostly warm where they live, but it can get cold in the winter. Once or twice, there was even a little snow! The crops do not grow in winter, which is why spring and summer are important. The Ramirez family grows as much food as possible while the weather is warm. Maria and Angela like the warm weather because they can play outside and ride the horses.

During the week, Maria and Angela get up very early to do their chores before school. Their job is to feed the animals. Maria likes to sleep late, however, and Angela often has to wake her up.

"Get up! We have to do our chores!" Angela commands, shaking her older sister.

"Can't you do them?" Maria yawns.

"We both have to help!" says Angela.

The girls go out to the barn, where they feed the dogs first. The dogs, hearing the girls' footsteps, rush to their bowls. Maria pours them water while Angela pets them.

Next, the girls feed the horses. They put oats in their stalls and give them carrots. Once in a while, they treat the horses to sugar cubes. Angela holds the sugar in her open hand so that the horse can eat it. "It tickles," she laughs.

Next to be fed are the chickens. Their food is scattered on the ground.

Last, the girls put food in big tubs for the pigs. Because the pigs are messy when they eat, the girls stand out of the way.

The biggest crop the Ramirez family grows is wheat. It grows best in a dry, hot climate. When the wheat ripens in the late summer, the Ramirezes harvest it.

The wheat grain is taken back to the barn in trucks so it can then be sold to a mill. Selling items grown on the ranch is an important part of Mr. Ramirez's occupation.

The Ramirezes' wheat is used in many foods. Bread, cereal, and cookies all can be made with wheat! Other crops grow on the ranch too. Corn and soybean seeds are planted in early spring. If there is enough rain and sun, the crops will grow large.

Maria and Angela like to grow food. They also like to eat the food their family grows. When they get home from school, they always make peanut butter and jelly sandwiches.

"Maria, did Papi make this bread?" asks Angela.

"Not quite, but he grew the wheat that was used to make it. Our wheat grain went to the mill, and the mill made the flour for the bread," says Maria.

"Did Papi make this peanut butter?"

"We don't grow peanuts!" laughs Maria.

"What about the jelly? Did we grow it?" presses Angela.

"No, but somebody grew the strawberries to make it, and then somebody turned the strawberries into jelly."

"It tastes good, no matter who made it!" smiles Angela.

Another one of the girls' chores is to brush the horses. Some days, they like to put flowers in the horses' manes. Because the dogs sometimes make a mess, the girls also have to make sure the barn is neat.

"Sit, Mimi!" Maria orders one of the dogs.

Mimi runs around the barn causing madness. He knocks over haystacks that are used to feed their cows.

"Where is the new puppy?" asks Angela.

The girls look all over the barn. Angela checks the corners, while Maria looks in the horse stalls. They look behind the hay as Mimi follows them all around the barn.

"Here, puppy!" calls Maria.

The girls hear a bark as the puppy runs in and jumps onto the hay.

"There he is! He was hiding!" they laugh.

Sometimes Maria and Angela like to visit the cows. Cattle are very important to the ranch. The family raises cows and sells them at the market.

This year the town is going to hold a livestock show at the market.

The girls are excited that they get to choose their own cows for the livestock show. They walk to the field near the house and watch the cows eating the grass.

"Which cow are you going to pick?" asks Angela.

"I don't know. I like the nice brown one with white spots," says Maria.

"I like it too," says Angela, petting a small black cow. "This one also looks sweet!"

"This cow has big spots," Maria notices. "She is pretty just like the black one. Let's bring both to the show!"

Raising the cows is hard work. They are kept in pastures on the ranch. They are well-fed, so they grow big enough to sell at the market. In late spring, the cows are moved to a different pasture.

Moving the cattle is not easy! Mr. Ramirez and Uncle Leo use the ranch horses to help. The cows go where the horses lead them. Uncle Leo also drives a truck behind the cows as they move. Sometimes Maria and Angela ride along with Uncle Leo in his truck.

"Uncle, why are we moving the cows from one field to another?" asks Maria.

"They've eaten all the grass in one pasture," answers Uncle Leo. "We need to move them to a new field with more grass."

Soon, the cows are ready to go to market. Maria and Angela watch their father weigh the cows. He is happy that they are big. The bigger cows sell faster, he tells them. Maria and Angela show their father the cows they have chosen for the livestock show, but Angela looks worried.

"Papi, will someone try to buy my cow?"

"No," says Mr. Ramirez. "Your cow is just for showing. People will look at her and admire her, but your cow is not for sale!"

"Good," says Angela. "I want to keep her!"

The day of the livestock show arrives.
Angela has named the brown cow Linda.
Linda has a pink ribbon tied around her neck.
Angela brushes her and makes her coat shiny.
Maria's cow, Princess, is a small and shy cow.
Maria brushes Princess's coat before they
leave.

"Girls! Are you ready? We'll be leaving
soon," calls Mrs. Ramirez from the house.

"We're ready!" the girls call back.

Mr. Ramirez and Uncle Leo prepare the
cattle for the trip to market. It can be difficult
to load them on the trailer. Uncle Leo hooks
the trailer up to his truck. The cows must
be led carefully onto the trailer. Maria and
Angela's cows get in last. Uncle Leo drives
slowly. The cows are on their way!

Linda and Princess are unloaded at the show grounds. Mr. Ramirez and Uncle Leo take the rest of the cattle to the market, where they hope to sell many cows. Mrs. Ramirez takes Maria and Angela to the show tent. The girls lead their cows to the front. As they enter Linda and Princess in the contest, they notice a row of big blue ribbons. Both Maria and Angela want their cows to win a ribbon.

"Mami, who will win?" asks Angela.

"We have to wait and see!" replies Mrs. Ramirez, smiling.

"I'm scared, Mami. What if we lose?" asks Maria nervously.

"Then we'll try again next year! You should be proud of yourselves even if you don't win," says Mrs. Ramirez. "Your cows look great, and you both did very well!"

"We have a tie for first prize this year," announces one judge. "First prize goes to... Princess and her owner, Maria!"

"I won! I won!" squeals Maria.

"...and the other first prize goes to... Linda and her owner, Angela!"

"I won too!" cries Angela, clapping her hands together.

The girls hug each other and hurry to the stage to get their blue ribbons.

Mr. Ramirez and Uncle Leo have had a good day as well. A farmer from a nearby town bought most of the cows. All the others were sold one by one. Proud and happy that their cattle did well, Mr. Ramirez and Uncle Leo are also very tired.

"Congratulations, everybody! We had a big day," says Mr. Ramirez, driving the trailer home.

"Yes, we did!" agrees Angela.

From the trailer, the girls hear Linda's and Princess's loud MOOs!

"They had a big day too!" laughs Mrs. Ramirez.

Maria and Angela are tired when they get back to the ranch. It is already bedtime. They pet their cows one last time, showing them the ribbons they have won. Mrs. Ramirez lets the girls have dessert before heading to their room. They deserve a treat too!

The grown-ups also go to bed, because everyone has to get up early in the morning. The crops will need to be watered again, and the animals will need to be fed. More cows will have to be prepared for the market. Life on the Ramirez ranch is always busy.

Women of the West

In the mid-1800s, people from all over the United States moved west. Gold had been found in California. Americans came from all over in search of riches.

Women played a big role in the history of the West. They made money by washing clothes, cooking food, and weaving. They built new lives there. Some became cowgirls or writers, like the three women shown below. Others raised families on the ranches out West.

By the end of the 1800s, women of the West could vote. Western territories such as Wyoming gave women the right to vote before many other states did.

Annie Oakley

Calamity Jane

Willa Cather